30-DAY Guitar Workout

An Exercise Plan for Guitarists

Jody Fisher

Alfred, the leader in educational publishing, and the National Guitar Workshop, one of America's finest guitar schools, have joined forces to bring you the best, most progressive educational tools possible. We hope you will enjoy this book and encourage you to look for other fine products from Alfred and the National Guitar Workshop.

Acquisition, editorial: Nathaniel Gunod, Workshop Arts
Music typesetting: Joe Bouchard, Workshop Arts
Internal design: Cathy Bolduc, Workshop Arts

Cover photographs:
Jeff Oshiro (upper right)
Jordan Miller (lower left)

ISBN-10: 0-88284-846-1 (Book)
ISBN-13: 978-0-88284-846-4 (Book)

ISBN-10: 0-7390-3632-7 (DVD)
ISBN-13: 978-0-7390-3632-7 (DVD)

ISBN-10: 0-7390-3633-5 (Book & DVD)
ISBN-13: 978-0-7390-3633-4 (Book & DVD)

Alfred Publishing Co., Inc.
16320 Roscoe Blvd., Suite 100
P.O. Box 10003
Van Nuys, CA 91410-0003
alfred.com

b14184035

Contents

About the Author

Jody Fisher has worked professionally in virtually all styles of music during his career, from straight ahead and contemporary jazz to rock'n'roll, country and pop. He taught Guitar and Jazz Studies at the University of Redlands and Idyllwild School of Music and the Arts (ISOMATA). An active performer in the Southern California area, he still maintains a private teaching practice and is a Director of the National Guitar Summer Workshop.

Other instructional products
by Jody Fisher:

Beginning Jazz Guitar (video)
Chord and Scale Finder
Jazz Guitar Christmas
Jazz Guitar Masterclass
    (with Joe Diorio, Mark Whitfield,
    Ron Escheté, Scott Henderson
    and Steve Khan).
Rhythm Guitar Encyclopedia
Stand Alone Tracks: Smooth Jazz
The Complete Jazz Guitar Method:
    Beginning Jazz Guitar
    Intermediate Jazz Guitar
    Mastering Jazz Guitar: Chord/Melody
    Mastering Jazz Guitar: Improvisation
The Guitar Mode Encyclopedia

Introduction

Becoming proficient as a guitarist requires two things: 1) an intellectual understanding of music and the guitar; and 2) physical dexterity so you can translate your ideas onto your instrument. This book is about the latter.

You may ask, "Aren't guitarists too concerned about speed and technique already?" For the most part, yes. However most of us are highly developed in some techniques but embarrassingly under developed in others. Maybe you're a real speed demon but your hammer-ons are weak. Can your right hand ALWAYS keep up with your left hand? Are your fingerstyle chops great and your pick chops poor? Or vice versa? How about string skipping? Picking triplets? The list of skills possible on a guitar goes on and on. This book will help you develop a balanced set of hands.

There are several ways you can use this book.

1. Learn the warm-ups and go right through the 30-day course as prescribed.
2. Look for exercises to remedy specific problems you are having.
3. Work only on the chord exercises.
4. Work only on the single string dexterity exercises.
5. Just work on your picking.
6. Just work on fingerstyle technique.
7. Just learn the warm-up.

Start off by working on the warm-up exercises for three or four days. This will give you a solid foundation and get you into the habit of doing this kind of work.

Next, start tackling the workouts. The first time through this book, I suggest you spend a few days learning each workout. Make sure you really understand that day's routine and gain some facility with the exercises before starting the next day's program.

After you have been through the plan once you will know how to customize your workout time. Some of this material is very challenging. Feel free to make up your own variations on what is suggested here. These routines take a little time to learn and your lifetime to perfect. Look for consistent weaknesses in your playing. This will point you to the type of exercise work you need.

> ### *DO NOT SPEND ALL YOUR TIME ON THIS WORK!*
> Good technique is a means to an end—not an end in itself. Spend most of your practice time learning new material and perfecting the old. Every once in a while go on a massive technique campaign. Then grab this book, and get to work. Good Luck!

Section One
Terms, Geography and Reading Music

Before we get started with the actual workouts, we should get a few things straight. Nothing too serious, but we need to define a few terms and directions that will facilitate learning the exercises that follow.

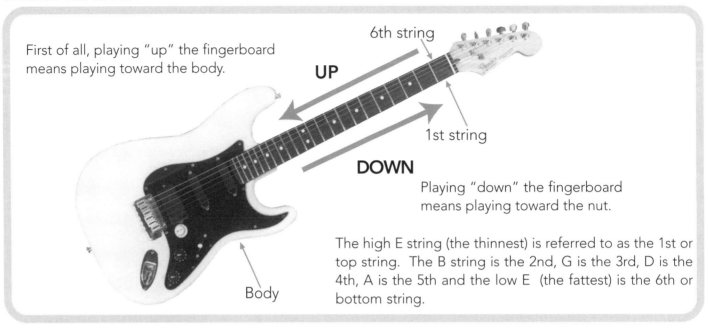

First of all, playing "up" the fingerboard means playing toward the body.

UP

6th string

DOWN

1st string

Playing "down" the fingerboard means playing toward the nut.

The high E string (the thinnest) is referred to as the 1st or top string. The B string is the 2nd, G is the 3rd, D is the 4th, A is the 5th and the low E (the fattest) is the 6th or bottom string.

Body

The left hand fingers are numbered like this:

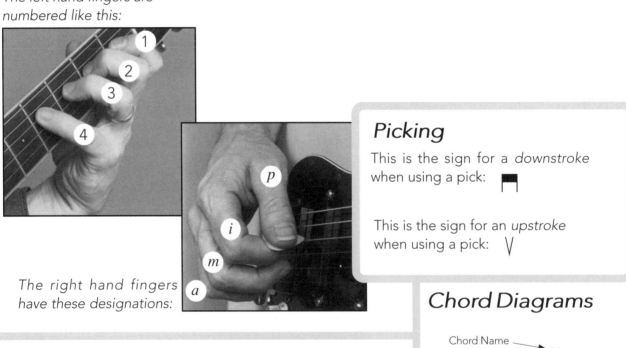

The right hand fingers have these designations:

Picking

This is the sign for a *downstroke* when using a pick:

This is the sign for an *upstroke* when using a pick: V

Tablature

Tablature is a system of notation that graphically represents the strings and frets of the guitar fingerboard. Each note is indicated by placing a number, which indicates the fret to play, on the appropriate string.

1st string, 10th fret
2nd string, 10th fret } -- Played together

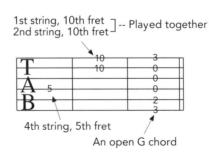

4th string, 5th fret

An open G chord

Chord Diagrams

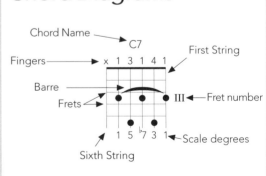

Chord Name → C7

Fingers → x 1 3 1 4 1

First String

Barre

III ← Fret number

Frets →

1 5 ♭7 3 1 ← Scale degrees

Sixth String

Pitches

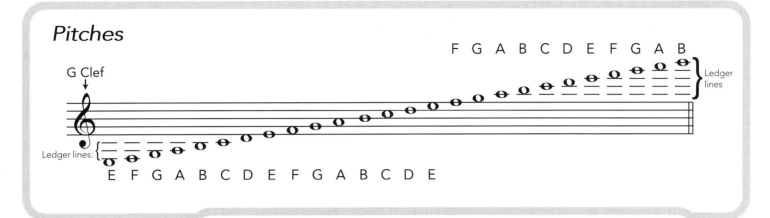

Measures and Bar Lines

Note and Rest Values

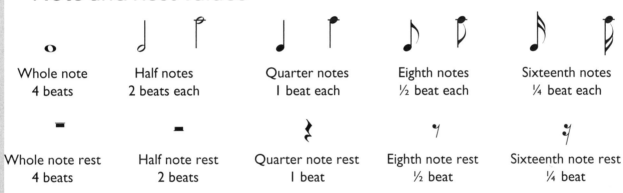

Whole note 4 beats	Half notes 2 beats each	Quarter notes 1 beat each	Eighth notes ½ beat each	Sixteenth notes ¼ beat each
Whole note rest 4 beats	Half note rest 2 beats	Quarter note rest 1 beat	Eighth note rest ½ beat	Sixteenth note rest ¼ beat

Time Signatures

At the beginning of any piece of music you will find the *time signature*. A time signature consists of two numbers, one above the other, which looks like a fraction. The top number tells us how many beats are in each measure. The bottom number tells us what kind of note gets one count.

4/4 ← 4 beats per measure
4/4 ← Quarter note ♩ = 1 beat

3/4 ← 3 beats per measure
3/4 ← Quarter note ♩ = 1 beat

The time signature you will come across most often is **4/4**. For this reason it is often called *common time* and is indicated by a **C**.

Roman Numerals
Shown with Their Arabic Equivalents

I	i	1	IV	iv	4	VII	vii	7	X	x	10
II	ii	2	V	v	5	VIII	viii	8	XI	xi	11
III	iii	3	VI	vi	6	IX	ix	9	XII	xii	12

Section Two Basic Technique

We're talking technique here! Pianists, violinists, sax players and all other instrumentalists learn early on that playing with complete control does not come naturally. Many hours of study and practice are necessary. But all the practice and exercises in the world won't help much if your basic hand position and posture are working against you. For some reason, many guitar players don't bother with developing good technical facility. We're not talking about developing speed—that comes later. We're talking about knowing how to sit, how to stand, how to hold the guitar, how to finger a chord, how to finger a single note, how to change chords and how to pick. Most guitarists seem to figure out their own way. Sometimes this works. Most of the time it doesn't. As a result, there are a lot of players working against themselves unnecessarily.

The ideas presented in this section are not new or revolutionary. There could be many differing views on this subject. Try some of these ideas for a few months before accepting or rejecting any of them. The workouts in this book will give you maximum results when combined with the following suggestions:

Your Strap

Always wear your guitar strap. Your hands should not have the job of "holding on" to your guitar—that's the strap's job. The strap frees your hands so you can play. Be sure to have your strap adjusted so that the guitar's height against your body is exactly the same whether you are standing or sitting. When you practice you are programing your body to react in certain ways. If you practice sitting down and the guitar is up against your chest, your muscles will move in very specific ways. If you stand up and the guitar is hanging down around your waist or knees, most of the programing goes right out the window. Consistency counts for a lot.

Your Posture

Yes, it matters. Every function of your body works better and more efficiently when your spine is straight.

So, don't:
- slouch
- lay the guitar flat on your lap (a slight angle is OK)
- rest your left forearm on your left thigh (a tough habit to break)
- push the neck out in front of you (you don't want to "reach" for notes).

Do:
- sit upright and slightly forward
- elevate the neck upwards slightly (with your head turned to the left, the fingerboard should be right under your nose!) Try to sit in the same type of chair every time you practice. Sometimes inconsistent progress can be traced to inconsistent positioning. Relax your whole body—arms too!
- breathe
- focus.

The Left Hand

The Invisible Thumb

In most situations, your thumb should be invisible to anyone stand-ing in front of you. Yes, some of your favorite players, from Hendrix to Farlow, have used their thumbs with success. There are very few situations where the thumb must be used. Generally, keep your thumb in "hitchhiking" position (pointed away from you) and place the ball of your thumb in the center of the neck. Your thumb will move around a bit while you play but try to maintain this position most of the time. The only time it is necessary to wrap the thumb around the neck is when bending strings. It helps stabilize the neck and provides a little more control.

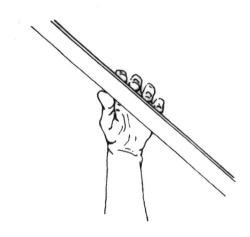

More Tips

Unless you are barreing or "rolling," your fingertips should be see-ing most of the action. Avoid using the pads of your fingers. Picture your fingers like the little hammers inside a piano and come straight down on the notes. Depending on the finger and it's position, you will sometimes find that it is more natural to use the side of your fingertip. This is OK. The idea is that you don't want or need to use much finger "surface." Playing with your fingertips will make you much more nimble and capable of nuance.

Go Lower...Lower

Try to keep your fingers as low to the strings as possible. In sports, this concept is called "economy of motion." If you are running a 50 yard dash and your arms are waving all over the place with your legs splayed in every direction, your time won't be very good. If you are keeping your arms and elbows in, with your legs moving in a straight and controlled mo-tion, you'll do better. By the same token, you need to have your fingers as close to the strings at all times. An inch and a half may not seem too far for your fingers to travel but at 200 beats per minute it can feel like a mile.

Short Stuff

Spend some time developing a nice staccato feel. Staccato means "short" or "cut off." Notes with a staccato feel generally have a strong attack with little or no sustain. When applying this technique to a fretted note, simply release the finger's pressure without re-moving the fingertip from the string. On open strings, we generally silence the note with either hand. Staccato is designated by a dot over the note ♩.

Long Stuff

To many guitar players, the term legato means playing with a lot of hammer-ons or slurs. This is only part of the picture. Playing with a legato feel generally means that the fullest value of the note is sustained until the next note is sounded. Practice playing ascending scales and patterns by leaving your finger on a note *until the next note is sounded*. The sound of the previous note is actually interrupted by the following note. This is primarily a matter of learning to feel and count and will take some time to master. Long, smooth lines are the sound of the pro. Uncontrolled, short choppy lines show amateur status.

The Right Hand

Holding the Pick

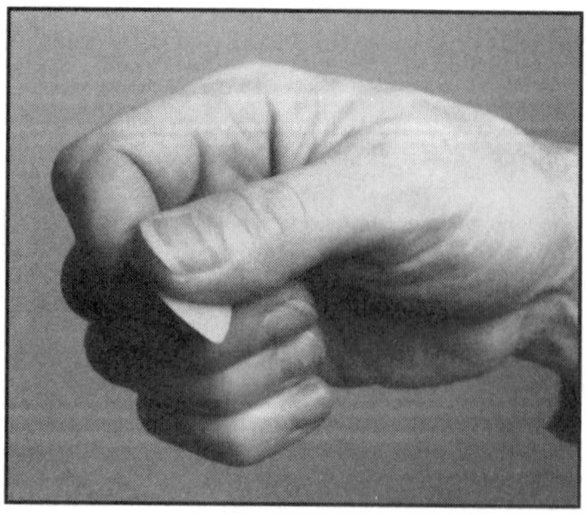

You should hold the pick between your thumb and index finger. There are so many hand shapes and pick designs that it is really impossible to tell you about the "one true way" to hold a pick. Generally, it is not a good idea to use very large picks. The standard triangular style or smaller is recommended. After a period of experimentation, make up your mind and stick with your pick. To a large extent, your pick is your voice—become one with it!

Fingerstyle

Keep your right arm relaxed and your wrist raised with your thumb and fingers "dipping" into the strings. Your elbow should rest on the body of the guitar. The thumb (*p*) should be in front (toward the fingerboard) of your other fingers. Swing your fingers back a little. Most of your finger motion should come from the middle joints. Your thumb generally plays the 6th and 5th strings. It would be very helpful to find a good fingerstyle or classical teacher to check your technique. Classical virtuoso Scott Tennant talks about right hand technique extensively in his book *Pumping Nylon*. If playing fingerstyle is new to you, it pays to get started the right way rather than having to "fix" technique problems later on.

Volume and Tone

These are more than just knobs on your guitar. You should eventually be able to adjust to any volume or tonal color with your pick or fingers alone! Try this test:

> Using downstrokes, play four slow quarter notes on any open string. Do it again, only this time make sure all four notes sound identical in terms of volume and tone. Keep working on it until you get it. Now, using all upstrokes, play four slow quarter notes on the same open string and match the volume and tone of the downstrokes.

Not so easy, is it? When you have mastered this, then do the same thing playing only two quarter notes. When you have that down, then go to a single downstroke followed by a single upstroke alternately. Be sure that the two strokes sound identical in every way. Try this at different tempos (speeds) and at various dynamic ranges (volumes). This is as much of an "ear" exercise as it is a picking exercise. Most players have fairly uneven picking techniques—they just don't realize it. This exercise will make you conscious of how your picking actually sounds and give you the means to remedy it.

Fingerstyle players:

You can do this too. If you pick single lines with *i* and *m* or as many jazz players do, *p* and *m*, the process is the same. Just strike the same string alternately until the volume and tone are the same. Practice slowly.

Files, Glue and Ping-Pong Balls

When you start to get serious about your technique, you can expect a little wear and tear on your hands, fingers and nails. First, take care of your right hand nails. Hold the right hand out in front of your face, nails away from you. If you can see a little moon-shaped nail edging just over the fingertips, this is the right length. Flatten the edge of the nail that actually strikes the string a little bit with a file so that the nail edge is parallel to the string. Then take a piece of emery paper and wrap it around the 6th string and rub your thumbnail against it. When the edge becomes smooth, do the same with the remaining fingernails. This "custom gauges" your nails to the string gauge you're using. Finally, buff the outer edge of each nail to make sure there are no pits or sharp areas that will effect your tone.

If you tear a nail it is easily fixed using super glue. Yep, you heard right. Squirt some on, let it dry and file it smooth. If you actually break the nail off, cut up a ping pong ball and shape a fragment to fit your nail. Whip out your trusty tube of super glue and your file and you're back in business. For split callouses or other tears on your left hand fingers—you guessed it, super glue. Don't put it on open wounds, but for splits and small holes, it works great. Be careful with this stuff, there are health risks if used incorrectly.

Other Thoughts

Swing Shift

Many lines played on a guitar require shifting from one position on the fingerboard to another. Look at this major scale fingering:

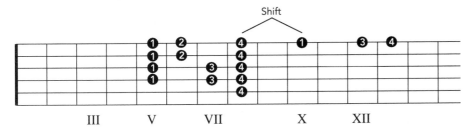

You can see that playing the final three notes of this fingering will force you to shift. You have to move the 4th finger from C on the 8th fret of the 1st string up to the 1st finger D on the 10th fret. It is important to practice this move until it sounds as smooth as if there were no shift at all. To hear what this should sound like, play C with your 1st finger and D with your 3rd. Play them back and forth, over and over. Now match that sound using the actual fingers the shift requires—4th finger to the 1st finger. Play both fingerings until they sound the same. If you are having trouble with this, slow down. Practice all shifts in this manner.

Slower...slower...slower

There is one cure for every technical problem on the guitar: *Slow down.* Almost everyone practices too fast. A single mistake means that you are practicing too fast. Always. When you are programming new information (songs, exercises etc.) into your subconscious, you want it to be right. If you make mistakes, you are also programming those mistakes or at least the mental pattern that it is OK to make mistakes. Practice a new idea until you can play it twenty-five times consecutively without a mistake. This may mean playing agonizingly slow, but when you can do this you will be ready to bump the speed up a bit.

In this section you will learn a great warm-up routine. If you are not in the habit of warming up before you practice or play, you should know that you are probably not playing up to your potential. Trying to play well without warming up is like trying to run a race without stretching first. You can do some real damage, such as causing harmful muscle strain or even tendonitis.

This warm-up consists of four separate exercises. Two for your left hand and two for your right. If you don't have time for a full practice session before your gig, this routine should warm you up just fine.

Warm-Up Exercise #1
Main Squeeze

This exercise should be done as slowly as possible. Play F at the 1st fret of the 6th string. Exert maximum pressure with your first finger and hold for a slow count of four. Maintaining this pressure, now add your 2nd finger on F#. With maximum pressure, count to four again. Add your 3rd finger to G maintaining the firm pressure with your first two fingers. Hold for four more. Now, while maintaining all the pressure play G# with your 4th finger and press hard.

At this point, maintain the pressure on fingers 2, 3 and 4 while you move your 1st finger from F on the 6th string to the Bb on the 5th string. Once again, exert maximum pressure with your 1st finger. Continue moving each finger over to the 5th string. Maintain pressure and hold for a count of four each time. When all the fingers are pressing firmly on the 5th string, your 1st finger will now move to the 4th string, and so on. When you finish on the 1st string, relax your hand (it will probably feel a little stiff) and rest for a moment before starting the whole thing again from the 2nd fret on the 6th string. Eventually, you should be able to perform this exercise starting from each fret on the 6th string. Take your time with this—it could take months to master this. The main points to remember are to keep the pressure on throughout the exercise and count very slowly.

Read the grids from left to right for clarification.

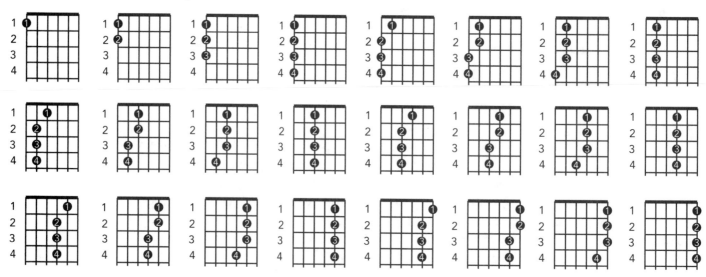

As you have just found out, this is a rather strenuous exercise. It will strengthen your hand and fingers and help you develop finger independence. Spending long slow periods with a single note will also acquaint you more intimately with the feel of your fingerboard.

Warm-Up Exercise #2
Alternate/Circular Picking (Tremolo)

A *tremolo* is a rapidly repeating note. This is an excellent warm-up for your picking technique.

What we are going to do is slowly play downstrokes and upstrokes alternately on an open string. When the downstrokes and upstrokes sound identical in terms of volume and tone you are ready to speed up a little. If it still sounds ragged, you are going too fast. When your notes sound even at this new speed, then speed up a little more. Keep doing this until a perfect tremolo is attained. The goal is to be able to maintain a steady tremolo for two solid minutes (yes, time it!). Spend two minutes on each string daily. The twelve minutes you spend doing this every day will give you more right hand control than you ever thought possible.

Some guitarists prefer *circular picking*. It is basically the same thing as alternate picking, but you pick in a circular motion. Straighten your thumb and reach forward on the downstroke. Bend your thumb almost forty-five degrees and circle back on the upstroke. Hold the pick very loosely. You thumb (*p*) and index finger (*i*) control all the action. You'll notice that at slower tempos the circle (actually its more like an oval) looks fairly large and at faster tempos the circle becomes almost imperceptible. Start slowly, making sure all the strokes sound perfectly even.

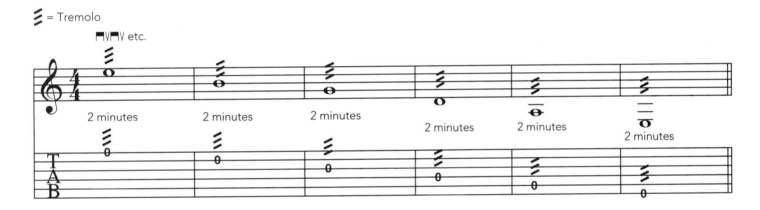

Warm-Up Exercise #3
Digits of Dominance

This exercise is designed to strengthen your hands and fingers and is to be done very slowly. Start by fingering the C at the 8th fret of the 1st string. Hold the note for four slow beats. Now barre the C on the 1st string and the G on the 2nd string. Hold for four beats, then barre three strings. Hold for four again then barre four strings. Continue this pattern until you are barring all six strings. **Important: no finger can touch any other finger throughout the duration of this exercise!** Then work your way back with five strings, four strings, three strings etc. This would be one round. The second round follows the same pattern only this time you use your second finger. On the third and fourth rounds, use the third and fourth fingers respectively. The slower you do this exercise, the more good it does. As your strength increases, try this on other frets.

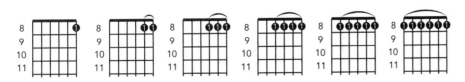

Warm-Up Exercise #4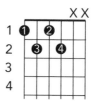
Fingers of Freedom

This is a right-hand fingerstyle warm-up. Start with this chord shape:

Sound each chord tone in an arpeggio with this fingering: *p i m a m i p*. Repeat and move the chord up one fret and repeat the finger pattern. Go all the way to the highest fret your guitar will accommodate and come back down. Repeat the entire process using this pattern: *p a m i p a m i.*

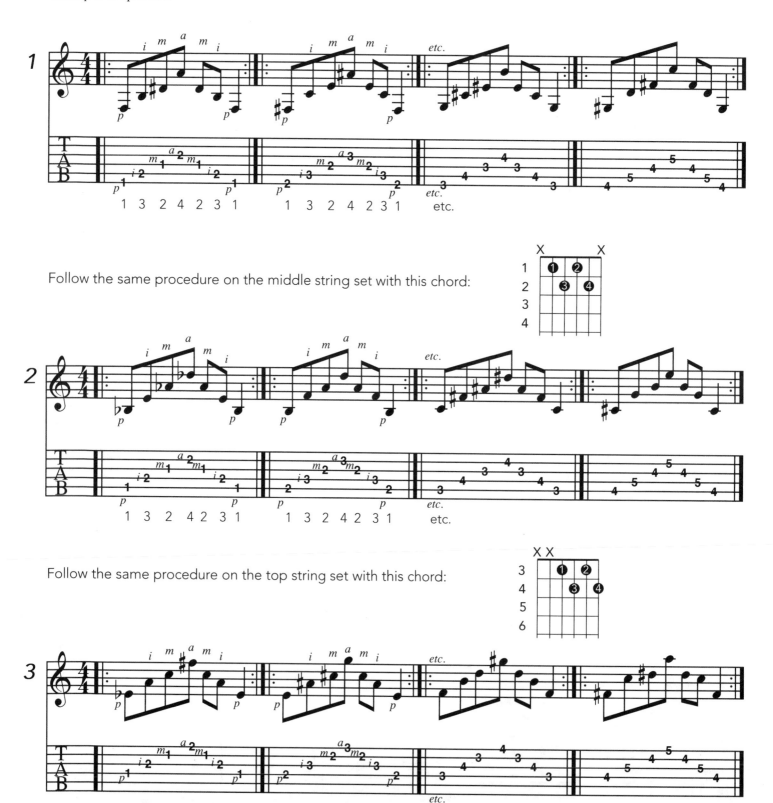

Follow the same procedure on the middle string set with this chord:

Follow the same procedure on the top string set with this chord:

The next step is to apply the *p i m a m i p* pattern to the chord on the low string set twice, then shift to the chord on the middle string set, apply the pattern twice, then move on to the top string set and repeat the pattern twice again. After you finish the pattern on the top string set, move that chord up one fret and repeat the picking pattern again. Move to the middle string set, repeat and finally shift over to the bottom string set and repeat the pattern again. Move up one fret and continue the pattern across the 3rd fret and on up the entire fingerboard and back down. Strive for an even sound from all right-hand fingers. Play only as quickly as you can and still make a clean sound.

Section Four The Workouts

From here on, its all hands on. There are thirty separate workouts. Each day begins with the four warm-up exercises you learned in the previous section. Each day's workout will include exercises (we'll call these Flexercises) that develop left-hand dexterity and chordal exercises (Chordiac Drills) to help with general chordal technique. Various approaches to picking these exercises will also be suggested. In most of the daily workouts, additional variations are also suggested. These workouts should improve your playing, maintain your technique and keep you prepared for most musical situations. There is a lot of material here and you shouldn't expect to be able to do all the exercises, with all the variations, every day. Do what's comfortable for you and try to go a little farther each time.

After you finish the book, return to Day One and progress to the next workout each day. How much time you spend really depends on how time much you have. Generally, try to spend equal amounts of time on each exercise. Imagine an hour-long practice session: after your warm-up, you may have forty minutes to spend on the workout. You could spend ten minutes each on four exercises. Or five minutes if you only twenty minutes. Some days you'll have plenty of time for this, and other days you won't. Don't beat yourself up or become fanatical over this—just do the best you can. Five minutes here and there can also be very beneficial.

Here we go....

Day One

Warm Up #1-4

Flexercise #1: Chromatic Scales

30 DAY GUITAR WORKOUT
1 2 3 4 5 6 7
8 9 10 11 12 13 14
15 16 17 18 19 20 21
22 23 24 25 26 27 28
29 30

The idea here is to play each note evenly in terms of volume and tone. Keep your left hand fingers low. Your thumb should be invisible, use only the fingertips and strive for a legato technique. We don't want to hear your shifts! Exercise 1a uses all six strings and 1b will give you practice with the chromatic scale along all six individual strings. Start slowly.

SECTION FOUR—The Workouts

1b

0 1 2 3 4 1 2 3 4 1 2 3 4 0 1 2 3 4 1 2 3 4 1 2 3 4 0 etc.

Chordiac Drill #1: Harmonized Scales

Memorize the following fingering for this harmonized major scale. Play the first chord and let it ring for four very slow beats. The idea is not to change chords prematurely. Count in sixteenth notes (one—e—and—a, 2—e—and—a etc.). Don't change chords until after the last sixteenth beat (the "a" of "4"). Then move all fingers simultaneously, up, over and down to the next chord. Practice this very slowly.

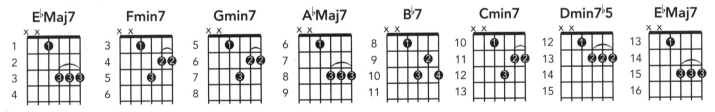

If possible, it is a good idea to practice this in all twelve keys. Transposing to the other keys is not hard if you know your key signatures and remember that the sequence of chord types is always the same:

I	ii	iii	IV	V	vi	vii	I
Maj7	min7	min7	Maj7	Dom7	min7	min7♭5	Maj7

The instruction to "practice in all twelve keys" will recur throughout this book. If you are comfortable with this, great! If you don't feel quite ready, try just a few transpositions. Work on developing this skill over time.

*8va means to play one octave higher than written.

Picking:

1. Practice Flexercise #1 using alternate or circular picking. Various tempos and volumes.
2. Practice Chordiac Drill #1 using all downstrokes, all upstrokes and alternating the two.

Fingerstyle:

1. Practice Flexercise #1 using *p* and *m* alternately.
2. Practice Flexercise #1 using *m* and *i* alternately.
3. Practice Chordiac Drill #1 striking all four strings simultaneously (*p i m a*).
4. Practice Chordiac Drill #1 using *outside/inside* technique.*

* Outside/Inside technique is simply plucking the two outside strings together on a down-beat and then plucking the two inside strings together on the upbeat. This example shows this technique applied to the harmonized scale in Chordiac Drill #1 on page 17.

Play Ascending and Descending

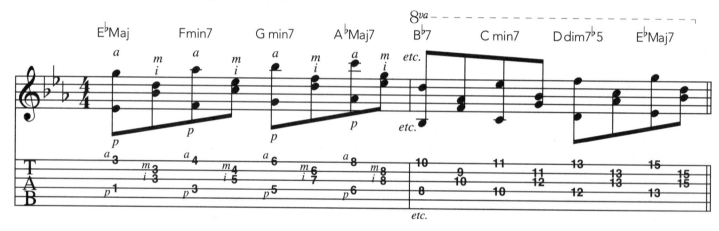

Try alternation.....outside/inside, inside/outside.

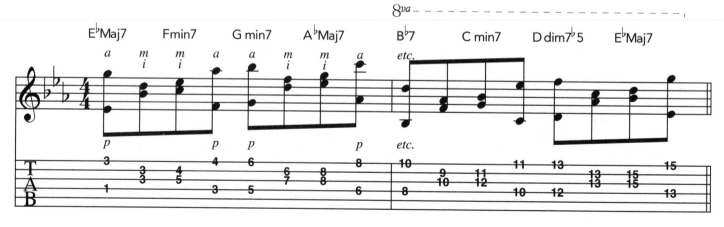

Day Two

Warm-up #1-4
Flexercise #2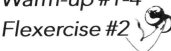

Play this pattern chromatically up and down the fingerboard on each string. Start slowly and increase speed. Strive for evenness and control.

Practice this pattern moving across the strings as well:

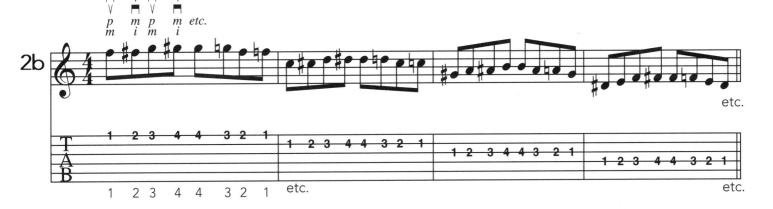

Chordiac Drill #2

Memorize this fingering for a harmonized major scale. Once again, hold each chord for it's full value of four slow beats before switching. If you can, practice this in every key.

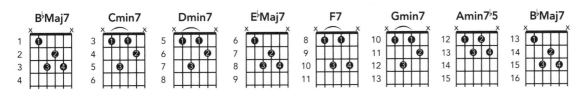

Picking:

1. Practice Flexercise #2 using alternate or circular picking. Vary the tempos and volumes.
2. Practice Chordiac Drill #2 using all downstrokes, all upstrokes and alternating the two.

Fingerstyle:

1. Practice Flexercise #2 using *p* and *m* alternately.
2. Practice Flexercise #2 using *m* and *i* alternately.
3. Practice Chordiac Drill #2 striking all four strings simultaneously (*p i m a*).
4. Practice Chordiac Drill #2 using outside/inside technique.

Day Three

Warm up #1-4
Flexercise #3

30 DAY GUITAR WORKOUT

1	2	3	4	5	6	7
8	9	10	11	12	13	14
15	16	17	18	19	20	21
22	23	24	25	26	27	28
29	30					

Play this pattern chromatically up and down the fingerboard on each string. Start slowly and increase speed. The open strings must be as loud as the fretted notes. Strive for evenness and control. Practice this pattern moving across the rest of the strings as well.

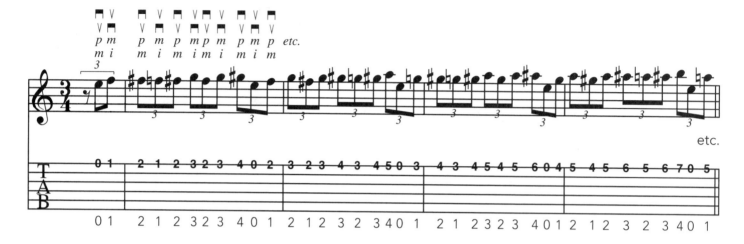

Chordiac Drill #3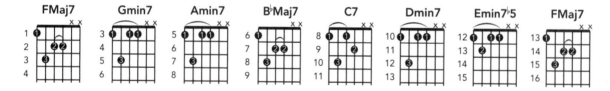

Memorize this fingering for a harmonized major scale. Hold each chord for it's full value of four slow beats before switching. Try it in all keys.

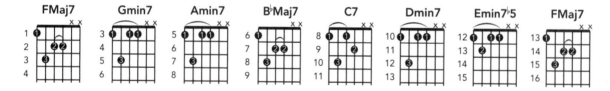

Picking:

1. Practice Flexercise #3 using alternate or circular picking. Vary the tempos and volumes.
2. Practice Chordiac Drill #3 using all downstrokes, all upstrokes and alternating the two.

Fingerstyle:

1. Practice Flexercise #3 using *p* and *m* alternately.
2. Practice Flexercise #3 using *m* and *i* alternately.
3. Practice Chordiac Drill #3 striking all four strings simultaneously (*p i m a*).
4. Practice Chordiac Drill #3 using outside/inside technique.

Day Four

Warm-Up #1-4
Flexercise #4

Play this pattern chromatically up and down the fingerboard on each string. Start slowly and increase speed. Strive for evenness and control. Practice this pattern moving across the strings as well.

Chordiac Drill #4

This is a melodic pattern played with the diatonic chords you learned in the previous three chord scales. The pattern is shown using the E♭ chord scale you learned in Day One, but you should also practice this with the other two fingerings you learned on days two and three. Remember, allow no space between chord changes—hold everything as long as possible before switching. Play it in all the keys.

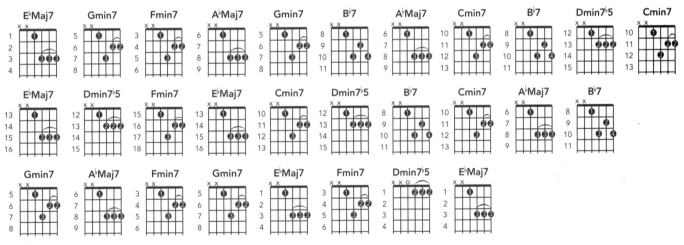

Picking:

1. Practice Flexercise #4 using alternate or circular picking. Various tempos and volumes.
2. Practice Chordiac Drill #4 using all downstrokes, all upstrokes and alternating the two.

Fingerstyle:

1. Practice Flexercise #4 using *p* and *m* alternately.
2. Practice Flexercise #4 using *m* and *i* alternately.
3. Practice Chordiac Drill #4 striking all four strings simultaneously (*pima*).
4. Practice Chordiac Drill #4 using outside/inside technique. You will have to change the example from whole notes to half notes here, because the inside-outside technique includes two motions for each note.

Day Five
Warm-Up #1-4
Flexercise #5

Play these patterns chromatically up and down the fingerboard on each string. Start slowly and increase speed. Strive for evenness and control. Practice these patterns moving across the strings as well.

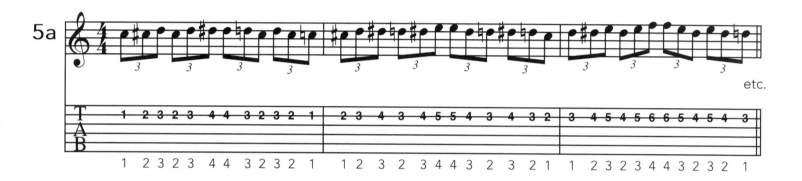

Chordiac Drill #5

Here is another pattern played with the diatonic chords you have been using. The pattern is shown using the B♭ chord scale you learned in Day Two, but you should also practice this with the other two fingerings you learned on Days One and Three. Remember, allow no space between chord changes—hold everything as long as possible before switching. Try this in all the keys.

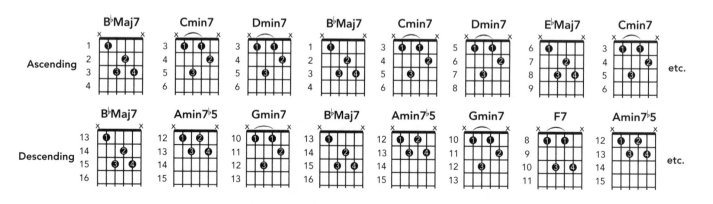

Picking:

1. Practice Flexercise #5 using alternate or circular picking. Try various tempos and volumes.
2. Practice Chordiac Drill #5 using all downstrokes, all upstrokes and alternating the two.

Fingerstyle:

1. Practice Flexercise #5 using *p* and *m* alternately.
2. Practice Flexercise #5 using *m* and *i* alternately.
3. Practice Chordiac Drill #5 striking all four strings simultaneously using *p i m a*.
4. Practice Chordiac Drill #5 using the outside/inside technique. You will have to change the example from quarter notes to eighth notes.

Day Six
Warm-Up #1-4
Flexercise #6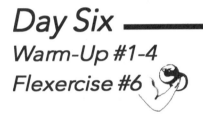

Play these patterns chromatically up and down the fingerboard on each string. Start slowly and increase speed. Strive for evenness and control. Practice these patterns moving across the strings as well.

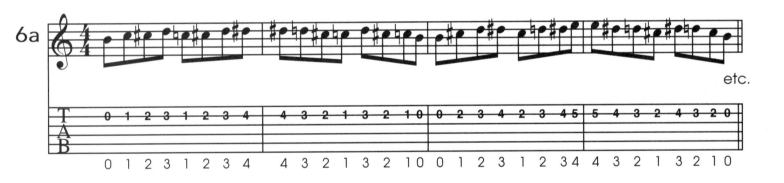

Chordiac Drill #6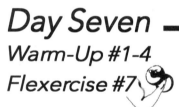

Here is another melodic pattern played with the diatonic chords you have been using. The pattern is shown using the F chord scale you learned in Day Three, but you should also practice this with the other two fingerings you learned on Days One and Two. Remember, allow no space between chord changes—hold everything as long as possible before switching. Try this in all keys.

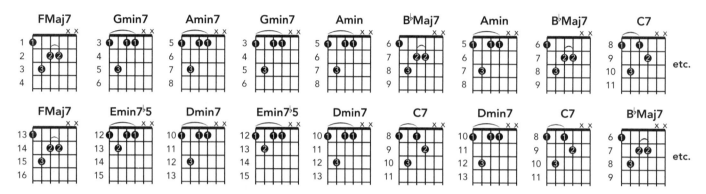

Picking:

1. Practice Flexercise #6 using alternate or circular picking. Vary the tempos and volumes.
2. Practice Chordiac Drill #6 using all downstrokes, all upstrokes and alternating the two.

Fingerstyle:

1. Practice Flexercise #6 using *p* and *m* alternately.
2. Practice Flexercise #6 using *m* and *i* alternately.
3. Practice Chordiac Drill #6 striking all four strings simultaneously *p i m a*.
4. Practice Chordiac Drill #6 using the outside/inside technique. You will have to change the example from quarter notes to eighth notes.

Day Seven

Warm-Up #1-4
Flexercise #7

Play these patterns chromatically up and down the fingerboard on each string. Start slowly and increase speed. Strive for evenness and control. Practice these patterns moving across the strings as well. As you can see, what we are doing is working on most of the fingering combinations. These can get tedious, which is why we work on different patterns each day. Just be sure that you are not playing too fast. Every note and rhythm must be accurate. Speed will come.

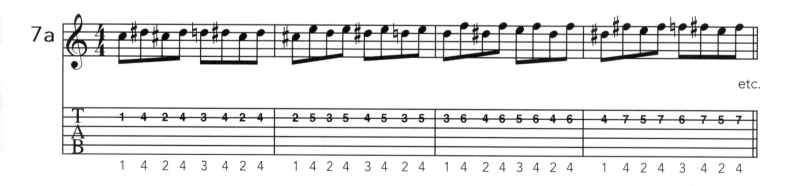

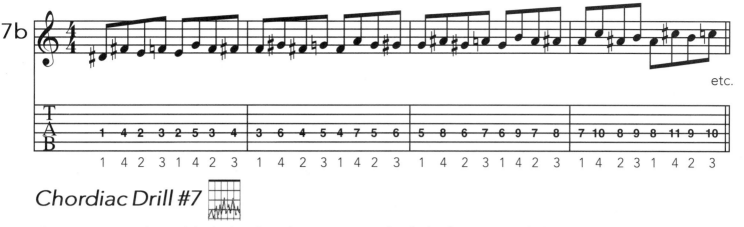

7b

etc.

Chordiac Drill #7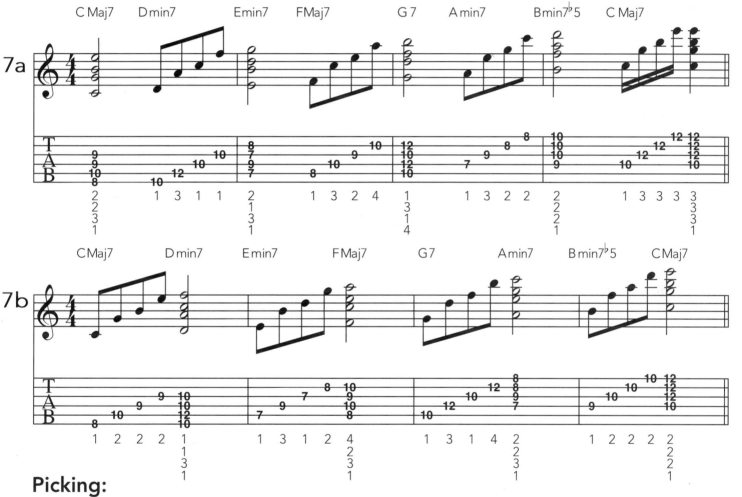

This exercise combines block chords with arpeggios. Check the fingering and play with clarity. Try to maintain a steady tempo. Switching from chords to notes (and vice versa) can be tricky. Practice carefully. Chords and single notes should be played at exactly the same volume. Practice in all keys!

Picking:

1. Practice Flexercise #7 using alternate or circular picking. Vary the tempos and volumes.
2. Practice Chordiac Drill #7 using all downstrokes, all upstrokes and alternating the two.

Fingerstyle:

1. Practice Flexercise #7 using *p* and *m* alternately.
2. Practice Flexercise #7 using *m* and *i* alternately.
3. On Chordiac Drill #7 strike the chords with *p i m a* simultaneously. Use *p i m a* on single consecutive notes as well. Strive to keep the single notes and chords at the same volume and tone.

Day Eight

Warm-Up #1-4
Flexercise #8

Play these patterns chromatically up and down the fingerboard on each string. Start slowly and increase speed. Strive for evenness and control. Practice these patterns moving across the strings as well. Concentrate and take your time.

Chordiac Drill #8

This exercise uses only block chords. The idea is to skip from chord to chord without missing any beats. Do not exit a chord early to get to the next chord on time. Practice slowly enough to accommodate these moves. Practice ascending and descending in all keys.

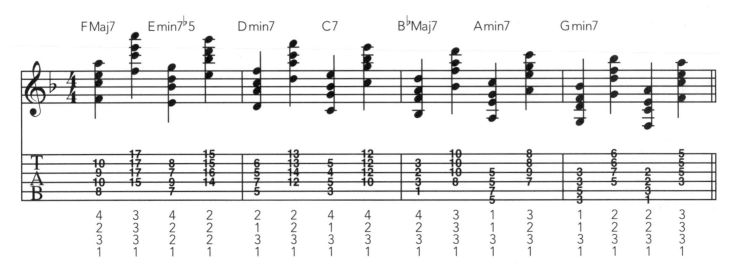

Picking:

1. Practice Flexercise #8 using alternate or circular picking. Vary the tempos and volumes.
2. Practice Chordiac Drill #8 using all downstrokes, all upstrokes and alternating the two.

Fingerstyle:

1. Practice Flexercise #8 using *p* and *m* alternately.
2. Practice Flexercise #8 using *m* and *i* alternately.
3. On Chordiac Drill #8 strike the chords with *p i m a* simultaneously. Keep all notes even dynamically. Try to imitate a piano, solidly playing all the notes at once. Practice at different dynamic levels.

Day Nine
Warm-Up #1-4
Flexercise #9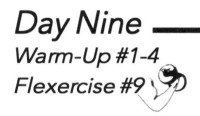

Play these patterns chromatically up and down the fingerboard on each string. Start slowly and increase speed. Strive for evenness and control. Practice these patterns moving across the strings as well.

Chordiac Drill #9

Here is another exercise utilizing the chords from the harmonized major scale. Once again, the idea is to skip from chord to chord without missing any beats.   Practice ascending and descending in all keys. Listen carefully.

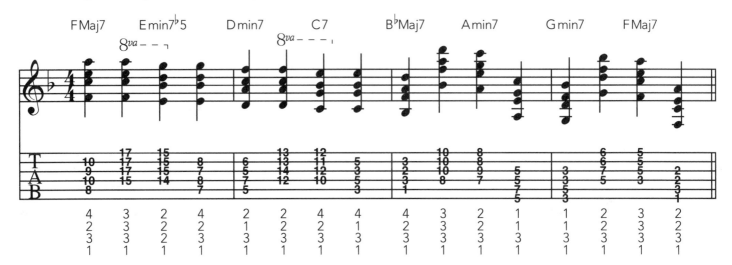

Picking:

1. Practice Flexercise #9 using alternate or circular picking. Vary the tempos and volumes.
2. Practice Chordiac Drill #9 using all downstrokes, all upstrokes and alternating the two.

Fingerstyle:

1. Practice Flexercise #9 using *p* and *m* alternately.
2. Practice Flexercise #9 using *m* and *i* alternately.
3. On Chordiac Drill #9 strike the chords with *p i m a* simultaneously. Keep all notes even dynamically. Practice at different dynamic levels.

Day Ten
Warm-Up #1-4
Review

Today is one of your review days. Practice each flexercise you have learned during the preceding nine days. Play up and down as well as across all the strings. This is also a chance to try some of the alternate ways of picking that you may not have tried yet.

Day Eleven
Warm-Up #1-4
Review

Today is another review day. Go back and practice each chordiac drill from the previous days. Remember to practice in all keys. Try new ways of picking these.

Day Twelve
Warm-Up #1-4
Flexercise #10

Here is an interesting triad exercise. Observe the fingerings. When you have played through the exercise as written, you have played the twelve major triads in cycle of 4ths order in one area of the neck. Each 1st finger shift on the 3rd string actually sets you up for the next move up the fingerboard. Once you have memorized the pattern, start again by placing your 2nd finger on the 2nd fret and moving up the neck from there. The picking is crucial, so follow the markings. This one's a burner!

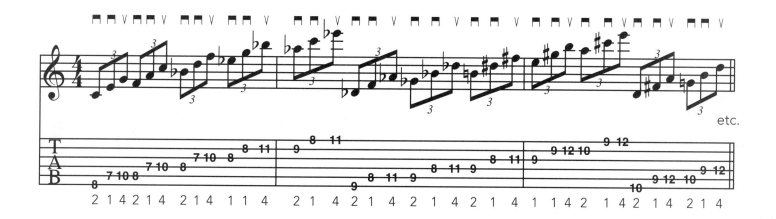

Chordiac Drill #10

Here is a chord stretching exercise. Start with the major 7th shape:

Then move each finger down one fret at a time starting with your first finger, then 2nd etc. The trick is to do this very slowly so you have to hold the chord down for a while. Slide each finger down without lifting off of any note. Travel from the top of the fingerboard all the way down to the first fret.

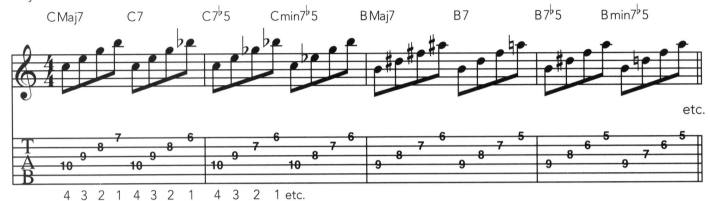

4 3 2 1 4 3 2 1 4 3 2 1 etc.

Practice the same way with these shapes:

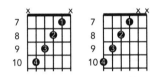

Picking:

1. Practice Flexercise #10 with this picking pattern: down—down—up, down—down—up, etc. Keep all notes even in terms of volume and tone. Practice this at a variety of tempos!
2. Practice Chordiac Drill #10 using all downstrokes. Then use alternate/circular picking.

Fingerstyle:

1. Practice Flexercise #10 using *p* and *m* alternately.
2. Practice Flexercise #10 using *p m i* repeatedly. Play evenly.
3. Practice Flexercise #10 using *m* and *i* alternately.
4. On Chordiac Drill #10, arpeggiate using *p i m a*. Keep all notes even dynamically. Practice at different dynamic levels.

Day Thirteen
Warm-Up #1-4
Flexercise #11

The exercise on the top of page 31 is a variation on the triad exercise you learned yesterday. We are adding the major 7th to each triad by playing the tone which lies one half step below each triad's root. Otherwise, the pattern remains the same. This will give you major 7th arpeggios in cycle of 4ths order all over the fingerboard. Observe the fingerings. Each 1st finger shift on the 3rd string actually sets you up for the next move up the fingerboard. Once you have memorized the pattern, start again by placing your 1st finger on the 1st fret and moving up the neck from there.

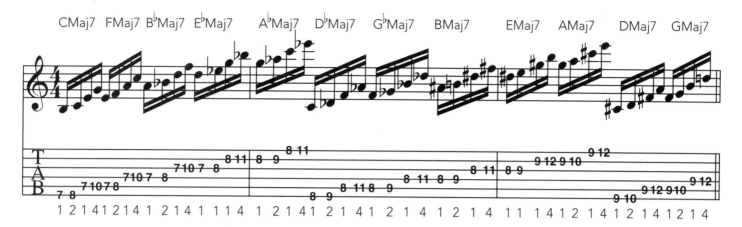

CMaj7 FMaj7 B♭Maj7 E♭Maj7 A♭Maj7 D♭Maj7 G♭Maj7 BMaj7 EMaj7 AMaj7 DMaj7 GMaj7

Chordiac Drill #11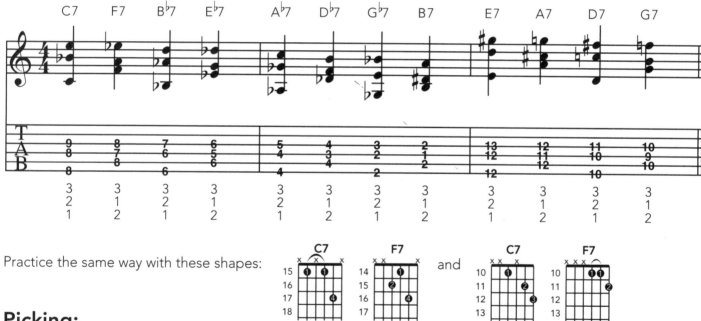

Following the same theme of traveling through the cycle, this is an exercise using dominant 7th triads. You are basically alternating between a voicing on string set 6/4/3 (6th string, 4th string and 3rd string) and a voicing on string set 5/4/3. Playing one, then the other, then moving down two frets and repeating the process will give you the whole cycle of 4ths over the entire fingerboard. Once you see the pattern with these voicings, try the same routine of alternating and moving down a whole step with these voicings on other string sets. Travel from the top of the fingerboard all the way down to the 1st fret.

C7   F7   B♭7   E♭7   A♭7   D♭7   G♭7   B7   E7   A7   D7   G7

Practice the same way with these shapes: C7   F7   and   C7   F7

Picking:

1. Practice Flexercise #11 with alternate/circular picking. Keep all notes even in terms of volume and tone. Try it at various tempos!
2. Practice Chordiac Drill #11 using all downstrokes, upstrokes and alternate strumming.

Fingerstyle:

1. Practice Flexercise #11 using *p* and *m*.
2. Practice Flexercise #11 using *p* and *m* alternately.
3. Practice Flexercise #11 using *m* and *i*. Play evenly.
4. On Chordiac Drill #10, play using *p i m*. Keep all notes even dynamically. Practice at different dynamic levels.
5. Arpeggiate Chordiac Drill #11 using *p m i, p* and *m* and *m* and *i*.

Day Fourteen

Warm-Up #1-4
Flexercise #12

These are *three-note diagonals*. The fingerboard can be divided into four string sets of three strings each. First, follow the pattern ascending and descending the fingerboard on the individual string sets. Then try crossing the string sets. In other words, play the pattern ascending at the 1st fret across all string sets. Then move up to the 2nd fret and play the pattern descending across the string sets in the opposite direction. Weave your way up and down the entire fingerboard. This is a little tricky, so go slowly at first.

Chordiac Drill #12

Over the next several days you will be playing diatonic chords built on 4ths (an interval distance of five half steps). The first group is on string set 1/2/3. If you can, practice it in all keys. Memorizing this sequence of chord drills will help you master the fingerboard.

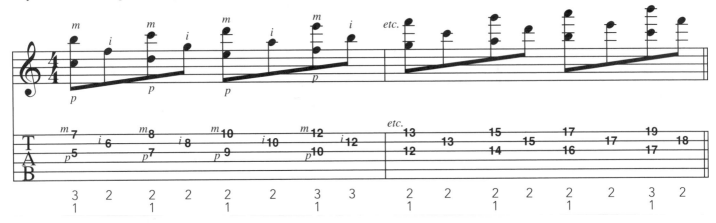

Picking:

1. Practice Flexercise #12 with alternate/circular picking. Keep all notes even in terms of volume and tone. Practice in various tempos!
2. Practice Chordiac Drill #12 using your pick and *a* for notes on the 1st and 3rd strings. Use *m* for the 2nd string.

Fingerstyle:

1. Practice Flexercise #12 using *p* and *m*.
2. Practice Flexercise #12 using *p* and *m* alternately.
3. Practice Flexercise #12 using *m* and *i*. Play evenly.
4. On Chordiac Drill #12, play using *p* and *m* for notes on the 1st and 3rd strings. Use *i* for the 2nd string. Keep all notes even dynamically. Practice at different dynamic levels.

Day Fifteen

Warm-Up #1-4
Flexercise #13

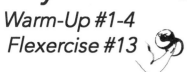

These are *four-note diagonals*. The fingerboard can be divided into three string sets of four strings each. First follow the pattern ascending and descending the fingerboard on the individual string sets. Then try crossing the string sets as you did for the three-note diagonals on Day Fourteen.

Chordiac Drill #13

Here are the fingerings for the diatonic chords in 4ths on string set 2/3/4. Practice in all keys. Memorize.

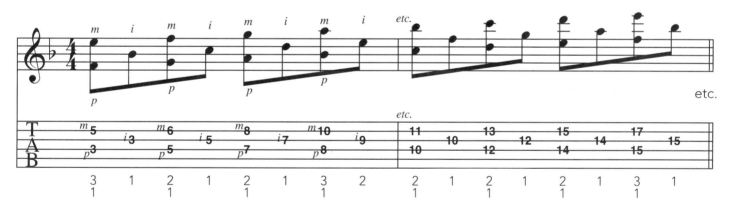

Picking:

1. Practice Flexercise #13 with alternate/circular picking. Keep all notes even in terms of volume and tone. Practice at various tempos!
2. Practice Chordiac Drill #13 using your pick and *a* for notes on the 2nd and 4th strings. Use *m* for the 3rd string.

Fingerstyle:

1. Practice Flexercise #13 using *p* and *m*.
2. Practice Flexercise #13 using *p* and *m* alternately.
3. Practice Flexercise #13 using *m* and *i*. Play evenly.
4. On Chordiac Drill #13, play using *p* and *m* for notes on the second and fourth strings. Use *i* for the 3rd string. Keep all notes even dynamically. Practice at different dynamic levels.

Day Sixteen

Warm-Up #1-4
Flexercise #14

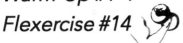

This is an exercise that will increase the span between the first two fingers of your left hand. Simply read across the guitar grids from left to right and then continue down the fingerboard. One move needs explanation: When you place your 4th finger down, your 1st finger slides back one fret as all other fingers remain where they are. This is done as *one motion*. It is as if your 1st finger is shot backward by placing your 4th finger down. This position is then held for a slow count of four. *Decrease* speed as you become more efficient with this. Start on the 9th fret of each string and slowly work your way down.

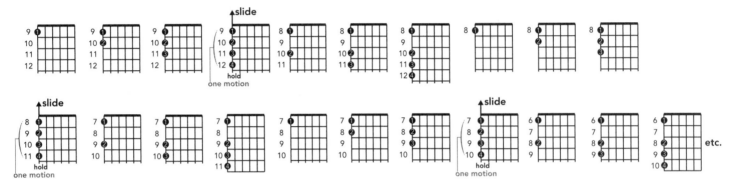

Chordiac Drill #14

Here are the fingerings for the diatonic chords in 4ths on string set 3/4/5. Practice in all keys. Memorize.

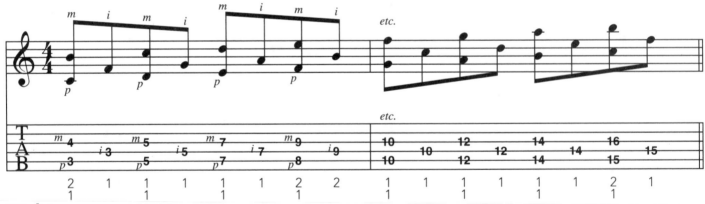

Picking:

1. Practice Flexercise #14 with alternate/circular picking. Keep all notes even in terms of volume and tone.
2. Practice Chordiac Drill #14 using your pick and *a* for notes on the 3rd and 5th strings. Use *m* for the 4th string.

Fingerstyle:

1. Practice Flexercise #14 using *p* and *m*.
2. Practice Flexercise #14 using *p* and *m* alternately.
3. Practice Flexercise #14 using *m* and *i*. Play evenly.
4. On Chordiac Drill #14, play using *p* and *m* for notes on the 3rd and 5th strings. Use *i* for the 4th string. Keep all notes even dynamically. Practice at different dynamic levels.

Day Seventeen

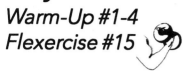

Warm-Up #1-4
Flexercise #15

Here is an exercise that uses ascending and descending minor 7th arpeggios. Continue up and down the fingerboard on each string set. The picking is the main point. Watch the fingering and strive for a smooth sound.

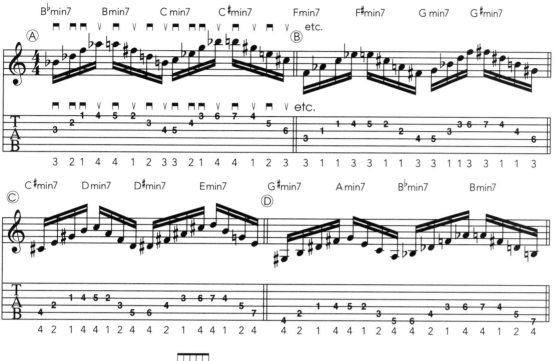

Chordiac Drill #15

Below are the fingerings for the diatonic chords in 4ths on string set 4/5/6. Practice in all keys. Memorize.

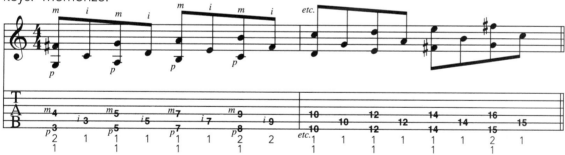

Picking:

1. Practice down—down—down—up on ascending patterns and down—up—down—up on descending patterns.
2. Practice Flexercise #15 with alternate/circular picking. Keep all notes even in terms of volume and tone.
3. Practice Chordiac Drill #15 using your pick and *a* for notes on the 4th and 6th strings. Use *m* for the 5th string.

Fingerstyle:

1. Practice Flexercise #15 using *p* and *m*.
2. Practice Flexercise #15 using *p* and *m* alternately.
3. Practice Flexercise #15 using *m* and *i*. Play evenly.
4. On Chordiac Drill #14, play using *p* and *m* for notes on the 4th for the 5th string. Keep all notes even dynamically. Practice at different dynamic levels.

Day Eighteen

Warm-Up #1-4
Flexercise #16

This exercise will help you with a technique known as the *roll*. When you have to move from one note to another on the same fret of an adjacent string, it is much more efficient to roll into that second note than to lift your finger off the first note and then place it on the next. To achieve an ascending roll, the first note is played with your fingertip. The second note is fingered by collapsing the top knuckle of the same finger so that the pad is covering the note on the adjacent string. Do not let the first note sustain through the second— just release a little pressure from the first note. A descending roll is accomplished by playing the higher note with the pad of your finger and "standing" that finger up (snapping the top knuckle into place) so that the second note is being played with the fingertip. Practice this exercise on all frets as the string tension changes from one location to another. Practice slowly and keep your eye on what you are doing.

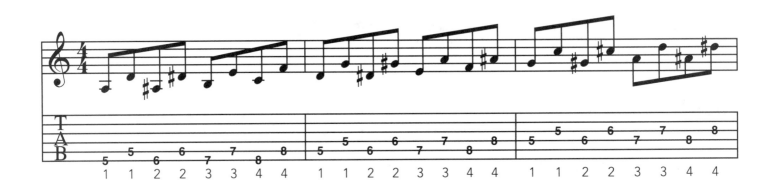

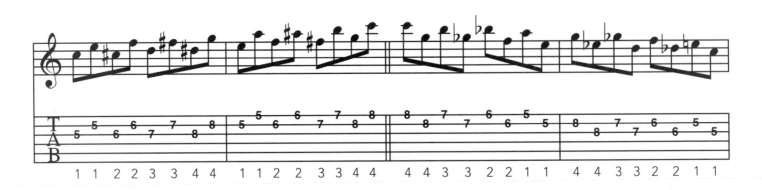

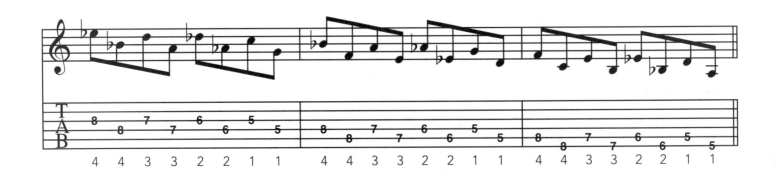

Chordiac Drill #16

Here is an exercise that will also give you some cool chord licks. The following is constructed from the intervals of tritones (three whole steps) and 4ths. By moving the tritone down by half steps, you are actually playing dominant chords around the cycle of 4ths. Practice this from the highest point your fingerboard will accommodate and travel down and then back up.

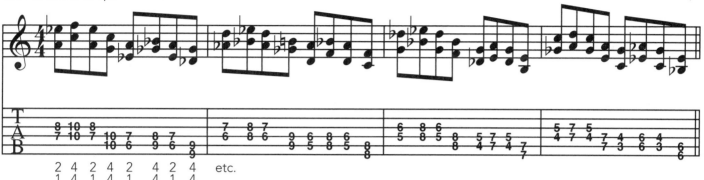

Picking:

1. Practice Flexercise #16 with all down strokes and then all upstrokes.
2. Practice Flexercise #16 with alternate/circular picking. Keep all notes even in terms of volume and tone.
3. Practice Chordiac Drill #16 using all downstrokes, all upstrokes and then alternate the two.

Fingerstyle:

1. Practice Flexercise #16 using *p* and *m*.
2. Practice Flexercise #16 using *m* and *i*. Play evenly.
3. On Chordiac Drill #16 use *i* and *m*.
4. On Chordiac Drill #16 try using your thumb.

Day Nineteen
Warm-Up #1-4
Review

Today is one of your review days. Practice each Flexercise you have learned since Day Twelve. Play up and down as well as across all the strings. This is also a chance to try some of the alternate ways of picking that you may not have tried yet.

Day Twenty
Warm-Up #1-4
Review

Today is another review day. Go back and practice each chordiac drill from Day Twelve. Remember to practice in all keys. Try new ways of picking these.

Day Twenty-One

Warm-Up #1-4

Flexercise #17

Now we will deal with hammer-ons. Be sure to play with the fingertips only. The goal is to make the hammered note(s) as loud as the picked (or plucked) note. Repeat over and over on all frets and all strings.

H = Hammer-on

Chordiac Drill #17

Chord etudes are great for developing outstanding chord technique. The remaining Chordiac Drills are four measure etudes. Take these very slowly. Most students find these fairly difficult. Just do your best until you have mastered them.

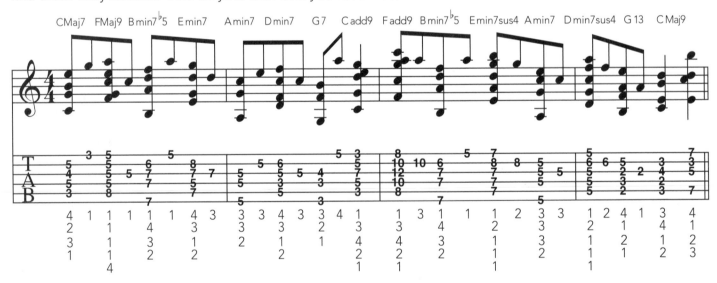

Picking:

1. Practice Flexercise #17 with all down strokes and then all upstrokes.
2. Practice Flexercise #17 with alternate/circular picking. Keep all notes even in terms of volume and tone.
3. Practice Chordiac Drill #17 using all downstrokes, all upstrokes and then alternate the two.

Fingerstyle:

1. Practice Flexercise #17 using *p* and *m*.
2. Practice Flexercise #17 using *m* and *i*. Play evenly.
3. Practice Chordiac Drill #17 using *p i m a* simultaneously or slightly arpeggiated.

Day Twenty-Two
Warm-Up #1-4
Flexercise #18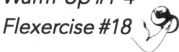

Here is some pull-off work. Once again, be sure to play with your fingertips. Make the pulled-off notes as loud as the picked (or plucked) note. Repeat on all frets and all strings.

P = Pull-off

Chordiac Drill #18

Here is the second chord etude. First get familiar with the chords individually. Then try putting them all together.

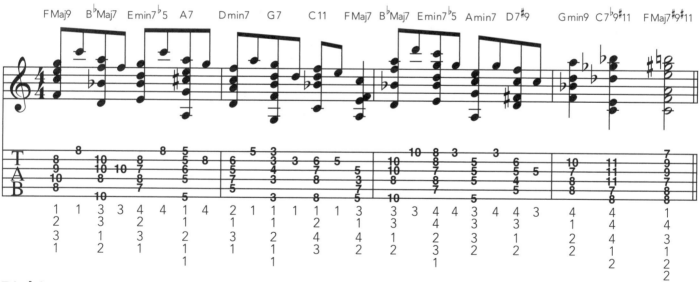

Picking:
1. Practice Flexercise #18 with all down strokes and then all upstrokes.
2. Practice Flexercise #18 with alternate/circular picking. Keep all notes even in terms of volume and tone.
3. Practice Chordiac Drill #18 using all downstrokes, all upstrokes and then alternate the two.

Fingerstyle:
1. Practice Flexercise #18 using *p* and *m*.
2. Practice Flexercise #18 using *m* and *i*. Play evenly.
3. Practice Chordiac Drill #18 using *p i m a* simultaneously or slightly arpeggiated.

Day Twenty-Three

Warm-Up #1-4
Flexercise #19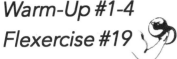

These exercises should help you with your string skipping. Play each one many times
Execute these patterns on string sets 4/2, 5/3 and 6/4 as well. Try different frets too.

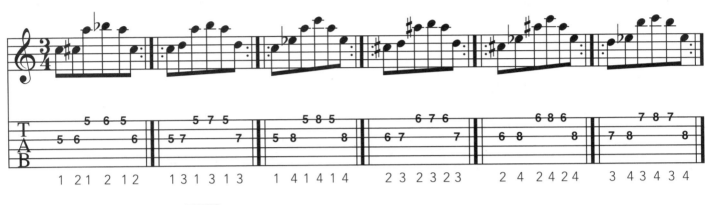

Chordiac Drill #19

Here is the third chord etude. Make sure single notes and chords are the same volume.

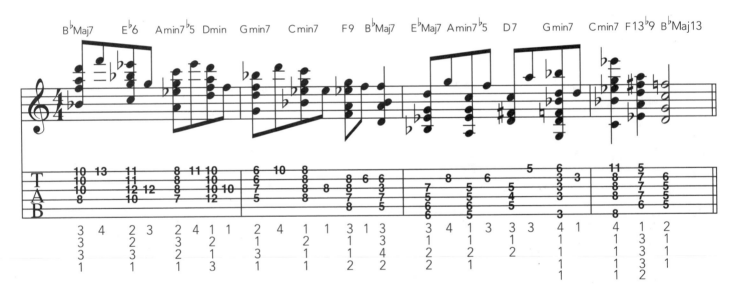

Picking:

1. Practice Flexercise #19 with alternate/circular picking.   Keep all notes even in terms of volume and tone.
2. Practice Chordiac Drill #19 using all downstrokes, all upstrokes and then alternate the two.

Fingerstyle:

1. Practice Flexercise #19 using *p* and *m*.
2. Practice Flexercise #19 using *m* and *i*. Play evenly.
3. Practice Chordiac Drill #19 using *p i m a* simultaneously or slightly arpeggiated.

Day Twenty-Four

Warm-Up #1-4

Flexercise #20

Play ascending and descending on and across all strings.

20a
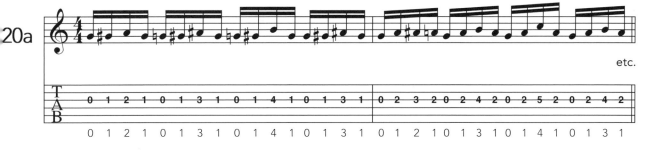

etc.

20b

etc.

Chordiac Drill #20

Here is the fourth chord etude. There are a few "stretchers" here. Take your time.

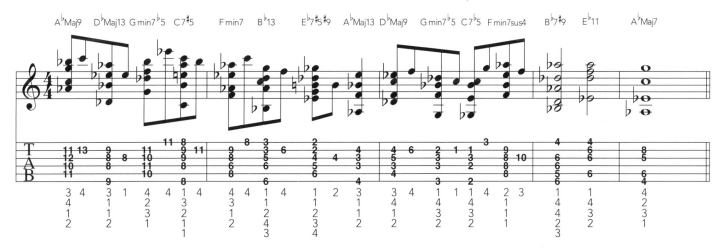

Picking:

1. Practice Flexercise #20 with alternate/circular picking. Keep all notes even in terms of volume and tone.
2. Practice Chordiac Drill #20 using all downstrokes, all upstrokes and then alternate the two.

Fingerstyle:

1. Practice Flexercise #20 using *p* and *m*.
2. Practice Flexercise #20 using *m* and *i*. Play evenly.
3. Practice Chordiac Drill #20 using *p i m a* simultaneously or slightly arpeggiated.

Day Twenty-Five

Warm-Up #1-4

Flexercise #21

Play ascending and descending on and across all strings.

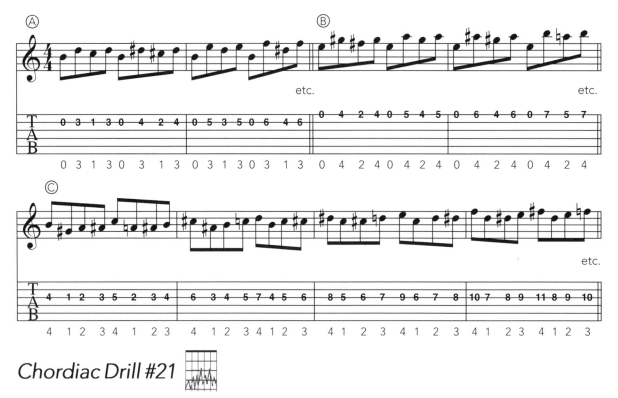

Chordiac Drill #21

Hands getting tired yet? This is the fifth chord etude. Take your time.

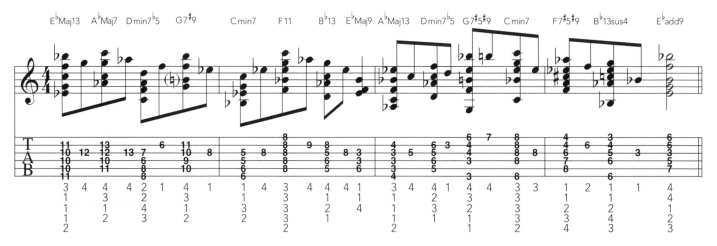

Picking:

1. Practice Flexercise #21 with alternate/circular picking.   Keep all notes even in terms of volume and tone.
2. Practice Chordiac Drill #21 using all downstrokes, all upstrokes and then alternate the two.

Fingerstyle:

1. Practice Flexercise #21 using *p* and *m*.
2. Practice Flexercise #21 using *m* and *i*. Play evenly.
3. Practice Chordiac Drill #21 using *p i m a* simultaneously or slightly arpeggiated.

Day Twenty-Six

Warm-Up #1-4
Flexercise #22

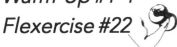

Play ascending and descending on and across all strings.

Chordiac Drill #22

This drill has more cool sounds, but you have to work for it. This is the sixth chord etude.

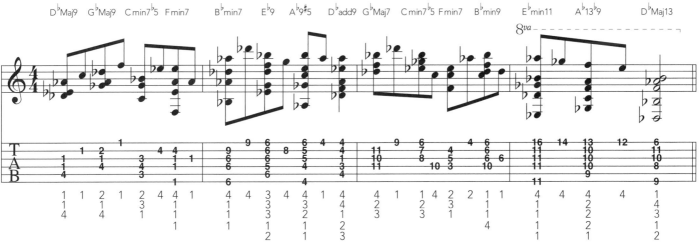

Picking:

1. Practice Flexercise #22 with alternate/circular picking. Keep all notes even in terms of volume and tone.
2. Practice Chordiac Drill #22 using all downstrokes, all upstrokes and then alternate the two.

Fingerstyle:

1. Practice Flexercise #22 using *p* and *m*.
2. Practice Flexercise #22 using *m* and *i*. Play evenly.
3. Practice Chordiac Drill #22 using pima simultaneously or slightly arpeggiated.

Day Twenty-Seven

Warm-Up #1-4
Flexercise #23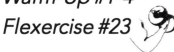

Play ascending and descending on and across all strings.

23a

etc.

23b

etc.

Chordiac Drill #23

Working on the lower register. This is the seventh chord etude.

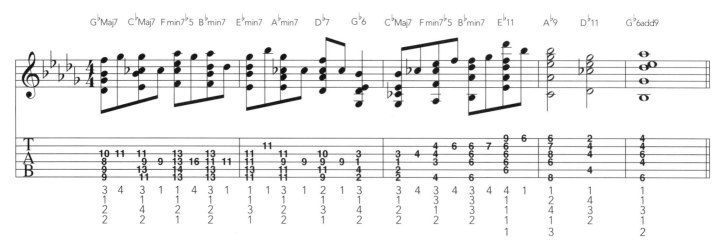

Picking:

1. Practice Flexercise #23 with alternate/circular picking.   Keep all notes even in terms of volume and tone.
2. Practice Chordiac Drill #23 using all downstrokes first, then all upstrokes and then alternate the two.

Fingerstyle:

1. Practice Flexercise #23 using *p* and *m*.
2. Practice Flexercise #23 using *m* and *i*. Play evenly.
3. Practice Chordiac Drill #23 using *p i m a* simultaneously or slightly arpeggiated.

Day Twenty-Eight

Warm-Up #1-4
Flexercise #24

Play ascending and descending on and across all strings.

Chordiac Drill #24

Welcome to the eighth chord etude.

Picking:

1. Practice Flexercise #24 with alternate/circular picking. Keep all notes even in terms of volume and tone.
2. Practice Chordiac Drill #24 using all downstrokes first, then all upstrokes and then alternate the two.

Fingerstyle:

1. Practice Flexercise #24 using *p* and *m*.
2. Practice Flexercise #24 using *m* and *i*. Play evenly.
3. Practice Chordiac Drill #24 using *p i m a* simultaneously or slightly arpeggiated.

Day Twenty-Nine

Warm-Up #1-4
Flexercise #25

Play ascending and descending on and across all strings.

25a

25b

Chordiac Drill #25

Take your time! These last few drills are very difficult.

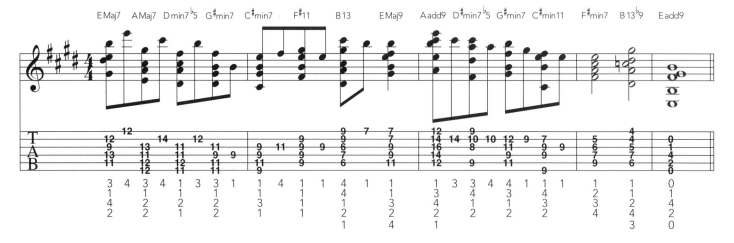

Picking:

1. Practice Flexercise #25 with alternate/circular picking.   Keep all notes even in terms of volume and tone.
2. Practice Chordiac Drill #25 using all downstrokes first, then all upstrokes and then alternate the two.

Fingerstyle:

1. Practice Flexercise #25 using *p* and *m*.
2. Practice Flexercise #25 using *m* and *i*. Play evenly.
3. Practice Chordiac Drill #25 using *p i m a* simultaneously or slightly arpeggiated.

Day Thirty

Warm-Up #1-4
Flexercise #26

Play ascending and descending on and across all strings.

Chordiac Drill #26

Be patient. Practice just a few chords at a time.

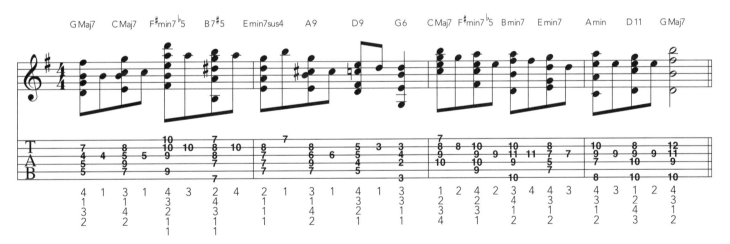

Picking:

1. Practice Flexercise #26 with alternate/circular picking. Keep all notes even in terms of volume and tone.
2. Practice Chordiac Drill #26 using all downstrokes first, then all upstrokes and then alternate the two.

Fingerstyle:

1. Practice Flexercise #26 using *p* and *m*.
2. Practice Flexercise #26 using *m* and *i*. Play evenly.
3. Practice Chordiac Drill #26 using *p i m a* simultaneously or slightly arpeggiated.